Lessons from A Young Soldier's Life

Finding Success in Life, Love & Career

The Remarkable Story of
Captain Sean Grimes, RN, PA-C, U.S. Army
The First U.S. Physician Assistant to Be
Killed in Combat

By Don Grimes

Table of Contents

Dedication:

This book is dedicated to:

- My kid brother Captain Sean Grimes, RN, PA-C, U.S. Army.

- All the men and women of the U.S. military and their families. You are giving more than any past generation has been asked to give.

- The families of our fallen warriors- I understand your pain   and sacrifice.

- Our warriors who were wounded in service to our nation. Please support them through the Wounded Warrior Project   (www.woundedwarriorproject.org)

- The members of the Society of Army Physician Assistants- thank you for your service to our country and for your love and loyalty to Sean.

- The American Academy of Physician Assistants and the PA Foundation- thank you for your loyalty to Sean.

- The staff and faculty at Michigan State University (MSU), Army ROTC at MSU, the College of Nursing at Michigan State University and Dr. Mary Mundt, Dean of the College of Nursing. Thank you for giving Sean the world's best preparation for a life devoted to healing and serving others. Thank you for your love and loyalty to Sean and his memory.

- My wife, Debbie, my son Scott and my sister Mary. Thank you for your love, patience and support.

- *The brothers of the Kappa Sigma fraternity nationwide for your kindness to our family and your loyalty to Sean.*

- *The Picatinny Federal Credit Unionin Dover, New Jersey for faithfully supporting the* Captain Sean P. GrimesPhysician Assistant Educational Scholarship Award given each year to a veteran studying to become a Physician Assistant. Their annual golf outing raises funds for Sean's PA scholarship.

- *All the people who knew and loved Sean. Thank you for loving our brother.*

For each book sold a donation is made to the scholarships my sister and I help set up to honor Sean. Companies, organizations and individuals are encouraged to make donations to either scholarship.

Captain Sean Grimes Physician Assistant Scholarship administered by the AAPA:
https://www.formsite.com/aapa2/form812474861/secure_index.html

Captain Sean Grimes Nursing Scholarship administered by Michigan State University (when you get to the MSU page you will enter "Sean Grimes" in the area that says "search for fund"):
https://www.givingto.msu.edu/gift/

Chapter 1

For Captain Sean Grimes, March 4th 2005 was just one more day to avoid being killed or maimed in the violent Anbar Province of Iraq, before flying to New York for two weeks of well-deserved leave. The highlight of Sean's upcoming leave was going to be a proposal of marriage to his girlfriend.

He had it all planned out. He would meet her flight at the airport and then take her to New York City for a fancy dinner. After dinner, they would walk down to Times Square and right there - in the middle of the flashing neon lights and excitement - he would get down on one knee and propose. A big family party in New Jersey had been planned for him and he was excited to introduce his girl, his future wife, to his large and loving extended family.

On March 4th 2005, the beautiful and smart young woman Sean loved was doing graduate studies in Vancouver, Canada. Her name was Leah Anne and Sean had met her at a party in Seoul, Korea and had fallen in love. She was an excellent match for Sean speaking flawless English and, surprisingly, German too - as did Sean (although her German was better!).

At that time, Leah Anne was working as a German to Korean translator for all kinds of technical and legal documents. Now, she was in a happy and excited mood, looking forward to flying to New York in a few days to meet Sean - her handsome boyfriend just back from the war.

I am Sean's older brother by 15 years and I woke up on March 4th 2005 with a happy heart – also looking forward to being in New Jersey for Sean's big party. My wife, young son, Scott, and I would soon be travelling there from our home in southern California and I was anxious to see my beloved little brother again.

I knew that 'Uncle' Sean, in full uniform with his chest glistening with hard won medals and badges, inspired deep admiration in my son, who would stare up in awe at his hero. I felt very proud of my brother and had spent hours working on the after dinner toast I was going to offer to Sean – and on the equally important second toast - welcoming Leah Anne into our family. I had imagined this happy family scene many times, illuminated by Sean's beaming smile as he sat with his arm around his girl.

In the pre-dawn darkness of March 4th, a group of Saddam Hussein loyalists left their houses in Tammin, a small village in the suburbs of Ar Ramadi and headed towards a dirt road near the canal. A few had shovels and several took turns carrying a heavy metal object shaped like a huge bullet. Their task was to bury the object under the dirt road before the sun came up.

Chapter 2

Sean was a Physician Assistant (PA), with training and experience equivalent to an emergency room doctor in the U.S. His unit was part of the U.S. Army's 2nd Infantry Division and had been deployed to the city of Ar Ramadi. He planned to spend this day riding in a Humvee on a Scout Platoon reconnaissance patrol, along with three other soldiers he liked and respected. His companions were the larger-than-life Scout Platoon Sergeant, the Scout Platoon medic, who had turned down a promotion to stay with the Scouts, and the vehicle gunner who had left a career in law enforcement to join the Army.

Some months earlier, Sean had made what would turn out to be a fateful decision, when his unit had first deployed from Korea to Iraq. He had decided to leave the relative safety of their base camp regularly and accompany day patrols and night raids with the Scout Platoon. He wanted to be closer to 'his' soldiers when they were wounded by gunfire or bombs and needed emergency medical aid.

To the troops, Sean was known as 'Doc' Grimes and he had a special bond with the soldiers he served with. He had once been a young enlisted soldier, too, and the troops understood he had been 'one of them'. They knew that Sean cared about them deeply - to the point where he was willing to leave the relative safety of their base camp voluntarily, almost every day, and put himself in harm's way to help injured men. (I say, 'relative', safety of the base camp because it was often the target of mortar attacks.)

The Scouts were also the Quick Reaction Force, so they deployed to every serious event that happened in their unit's area of operation. The Scout Platoon's daylight missions made them an excellent target for insurgents to shoot at or bomb. Sixty-four soldiers from the 2nd Infantry unit would die in Iraq during their 12-month deployment and many more would be wounded.

A sizable number of the dead and wounded were from the Scout Platoon. In a daily act of heroism that was repeated by members of U.S. units all over Iraq and Afghanistan, the young soldiers would 'saddle up' into their Humvees and go into the same streets where fellow soldiers had been killed or maimed in previous days. Sean was in his element in the field with a combat unit, because he loved medicine and he loved being a soldier working with other dedicated soldiers. He loved the soldiers' spirit, their courage and their strong dedication to each other, the Army and their country. In return, the soldiers loved him.

Sean was almost a poster child for the opportunities the military has to offer soldiers interested in medicine. After graduating from high school, Sean had enlisted in the Army Reserve and was trained as a Combat Medic. He then received an ROTC scholarship to pay for his degree at Michigan State University to become a Registered Nurse. After serving in Germany as a Registered Nurse, he won a place on the challenging Depart of Defense Physician Assistant program. During the entire time he served in an Army uniform, Sean had been encouraged by his Army medical mentors to apply for medical school and become a physician and he was planning to do that within the next three or four years.

I had spoken with Sean a few days before and heard the weariness in his voice as he told me of the most recent casualties his unit had taken. He had seen soldiers he knew and loved being killed and wounded. He had treated them under enemy gunfire in the field of combat and in the emergency room of 'Charlie Med' - the field hospital on his base camp. One heartbreaking story that Sean and others told me occurred at their base camp, when one of their ambulance units roared past and stopped in front of the field hospital. Sean ran to the ambulance and noticed the medic stationed on the ambulance had not begun the process of removing the wounded. Sean called out.

"Where's the medic? Where's the medic?"

The soldier driving the ambulance scrambled towards Sean yelling, "The medic was hit!"

Sean opened the ambulance and saw the wounded medic lying inside with his intestines pouring out of his abdomen. The medic had been shot just below the bottom of his protective vest. Sean jumped into the ambulance immediately, scooped up the injured soldier's intestines and held them in place with his bare hands. Finally, a stretcher arrived and Sean stayed with the wounded soldier, his hands holding in the intestines, until the soldier was in the emergency room and being rushed into Surgery.

Hearing the sadness in his voice at that moment chilled me. During the previous months of his tour of duty in Iraq, I had been telling myself that Sean would come home safely because he was a Physician Assistant, a medical type who would be safe in his base camp. As Sean's mid-tour leave approached, the missions he was going out on were getting scarier and more dangerous. I had read his emails about going on patrols with the Scout Platoon - being shot at and bombed and exchanging fire with the enemy - but somehow I was able to remain detached from the reality of the danger he and his men were facing.

The tone of his voice broke my sense of detachment. Without thinking, I asked him if he could stop going out on patrols with the Scouts until he came back home on leave. Maybe he could just "hang back a little", stay in the base camp for the next week or so. In a tired, but firm voice, Sean answered that,

"The troops can't hang back and my medics can't hang back, so neither can I".

On another occasion, a sergeant asked Sean why he chose to go out on the patrols and risk death or serious injury. Sean was quick to answer that his job was to take care of soldiers and, "The place where soldiers get wounded is in action outside of the base camp walls".

Sean also felt he owed it to the medics he supervised to share the risks they ran every day by going out with them and the various units they were assigned to. He thought of his medics as brave and smart young people who had volunteered twice, once to be soldiers and then to be medics.

One of the last emails I received from Sean told of a recent night raid he went out on with the Scout Platoon. On raids, one soldier would kick in the front door of the location being raided. The soldier who kicked in the door was especially vulnerable to being shot or wounded by a booby trap. Therefore, to be chosen as the 'door kicker' meant that a soldier was thought of as an especially brave trooper and was being offered one of the ultimate statements of courage. Sean's email told me the Scouts had offered him the chance to kick in the door of the suspected terrorist location that was to be raided that night. Sean accepted the invitation and 'Doc' Grimes became what many soldiers believe to be the first Army PA to be a 'door kicker'.

Sean watching the sunset at Camp Ramadi in Iraq after going out on patrol with the Scout Platoon

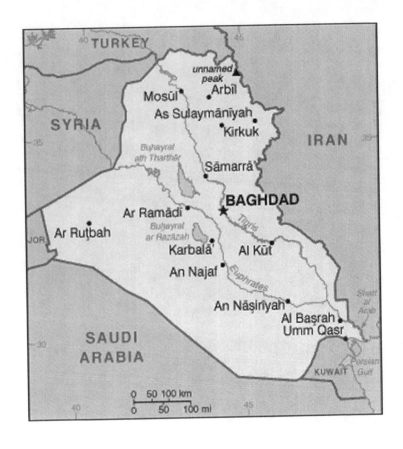

Chapter 3

Six month earlier, whilst stationed in Korea along the De-Militarized Zone, Sean and 2,000 soldiers from his unit were awaiting their orders for Iraq. Sean had volunteered for Iraq and then volunteered a second time to deploy earlier - so an officer with small kids could have more time with his family before it was his turn to leave for Iraq.

When the deployment orders for Sean and his fellow soldiers finally came through, he called me from Korea with the information and told me that his unit's deployment would be uniquely challenging. Instead of going out to relieve a U.S. Army unit already in Iraq, as was the usual routine, his group of U.S. Army soldiers were being assigned to reinforce and fight with the First Marine Division of the U.S. Marines Corps in Anbar province - the deadliest part of Iraq.

After Sean finished telling me the details of his coming assignment with the Marines, there was silence on the phone line. Finally, we both broke into laughter and I said,

"You know you're totally screwed if you're going to be fighting with the Marines!"

He agreed laughing, "Yes, brother, I believe I am totally screwed."

As soldiers, we both knew that the Marine Corps typically ends up in the worst situations around.

Sean spent his remaining time in Korea preparing to go to war and seeing Leah Anne as often as he could. Whenever Sean spoke to me about his sweetheart, there was something different in his voice. Sean was a unique and highly intelligent young soldier, who had traveled the world and I was happy to know he had found an equally special and intelligent woman with whom to share his future.

All soldiers going to war get two weeks leave and Sean planned to spend his two-week leave at my house in southern California. Most solders spend their leave having as much fun as possible, but Sean had a different plan. He was very nearsighted and had always worn glasses or contact lenses. Being nearsighted in a desert war zone has definite drawbacks, so Sean decided to have corrective surgery done on his eyes while on leave. The very common and pain-free laser surgery most people undergo was not suitable for Sean's purposes. He had always thought he might want to serve with the Army Rangers or Special Forces and go to the Army's special high altitude paratrooper school.

Jumping out of airplanes at very high altitudes can put tremendous pressure on a soldier's eyes and conventional laser surgery prevents a soldier from high altitude parachute training. Instead of the easy corrective surgery, Sean found one of the few eye surgeons who could perform vision-correcting surgery without using a laser, so he would later have the option of applying for high altitude parachuting training.

The surgeon was located just a few miles from my home in Orange County, California and had performed this special surgery on many Marines stationed at the nearby Camp Pendleton Marine Corps base. This alternative corrective surgery has one major drawback - it is a painful process that actually grinds down the

Sean and his nephew Scott riding scooters in Toys R Us store

cornea to achieve the desired vision correction and for a week after the eye surgery Sean had blurry vision, puffy eyes and pain.

Each morning, my young son, Scott, would walk into the Sean's bedroom, stand next to Sean's head and stare at him until he awoke. Scott would then softly ask,

"Uncle Sean, you want to get up and play with me?"

Sean would simply smile and say, "Of course!" and then get up and play with his nephew. Sean's pre-deployment leave was definitely not the usual way soldiers spend their last free days before going to war.

Chapter 4

Sean was born in 1973, into a very chaotic household situation. I was 15 years old when he was born and my sister, Mary, was 10. My sister and I considered it a miracle that the delivery room physician reported that Sean was completely normal and in possession of the correct number of arms, legs, fingers and toes.

We lived in a big house in a lovely suburb of Detroit that had great public schools. To people driving by our home, we may have seemed to be worthy of envy. However, inside our house, it was not so good and I tried to make sure that Sean and our sister were fed, clothed and insulated as much as possible from the chaos.

In 1985, I started a project in the metro Detroit area that asked people to send supportive Christmas cards and letters to U.S. troops stationed overseas or deployed at sea. I had been a young soldier once and was lucky enough to receive mail from home almost every day, but I felt bad for the soldiers who never got mail or any other indication that someone cared about them and their service to our country. My project grew rapidly and a few years later, I joined forces with nationally syndicated columnist, Dear Abby, an amazing woman with a huge heart. And thanks to Dear Abby, my Christmas project began appearing regularly in over 1400 newspapers.

Late in 1989, after I turned 30, I was able to secure a major sponsorship for my Christmas project and I quit my full time job and set up a small office in Lansing, Michigan. Southwest Airlines agreed to sponsor a media tour of cities in Texas and Arizona, where local groups and communities had agreed to 'adopt', a ship or unit for the holidays.

At the airport in those cities, Southwest created a giant Christmas card that was hung in a gate area so that passengers and employees could sign it and write supportive messages for the troops. I was going to appear on local television and radio shows in each city and was very excited.

I was just a week or so away from my much anticipated media trip, when my phone rang early one morning. I picked it up and my father said,

"Sean ran away from home. You have to come home and get him."

Time seemed to stand still as the words sank in. Sean had decided to run away from home, in what turned out to be an effort to force my parents to get their lives in order. I felt a tidal wave of pain and guilt sweep over me as, in that instant, I felt I had failed Sean by leaving him in that house.

I drove to my parent's home from where I called the police to file a missing person report. The desk sergeant sounded bored with me and dismissed my concern, telling me that Sean was "probably a typical kid who is mad at his parents for saying "no" to something he wants and is staying at a friend's house".

The cop assured me that he knew Sean would come home in a day or so. I disagreed with that assessment, without disclosing the unpleasant home situation Sean was dealing with and said

I still wanted to file a missing report. The cop said I could only file the report after Sean had been gone for 72 hours and then he hung up.

Fortunately, I had done some campaigning for the mayor of our town, so I was able to call in a favor when I called him and explained the situation. The mayor contacted our police chief immediately and within 30 minutes I got a call to say a detective had been assigned to our case and would be coming to the house within the next hour or so.

My parents and I stood silently in the kitchen, as the detective seated himself at the kitchen table and opened a small notebook. He began asking us questions about Sean and why he might have run away. My parents looked confused by the questions and told the detective that they had no idea why my brother had run away. Both of them assured the detective all was fine in our home and family. It wasn't the truth.

In the kitchen, I did not contradict what my parents were saying. After asking his last question, the detective closed the small notebook and put in his pocket. He said the police would begin looking for the car Sean had taken and suggested we began calling his friends to see if he was staying with them. Then the detective stood up, put his business card on the table and quietly left.

Seeing him walk out of our front door - without the truth - made me feel as if my final chance to save Sean was slipping away. I ran out of the back door and intercepted him as he reached his unmarked car. I blurted out every detail of our unfortunate home life that Sean now had to face alone. When I finished speaking, the detective just stood looking at me without saying a word. Finally, he nodded and said quietly,

"Oh, don't worry. I already know what your brother has been going through. I talked with most of your neighbors before I came to see you and they told me".

The next day, the police in a neighboring town found the car Sean had taken parked at the local Greyhound bus station and discovered that Sean was on a bus headed to New York City. Most of our extended family lived there and I hoped he was going to stay with some of them.

It was my job to find Sean and bring him home, so I flew to New York City straightaway. My upcoming media tour was not going to happen and instead, I had visions of having to bring my brother's body home to Michigan. I was sure harm would come to Sean as an innocent, young runaway in New York City.

That was a time when New York was a very troubled city - before Mayor Rudolph Giuliani had wrested control of the city and its streets back from the criminals, crazies and drug addicts who then seemed in control. My heart ached as I imagined Sean wandering the streets of New York feeling alone, unloved and abandoned by everyone - especially me.

I spent my first two days in New York looking for Sean, or his body. With a supply of recent photos of Sean, I visited or called runaway shelters, hospital emergency rooms and the morgue. I also went to the main bus terminal where Sean's bus would have arrived. The bus terminal is owned and operated by the Port Authority of New York & New Jersey, a government agency.

Back then the main bus terminal was a tough place. I went there and met with the detectives who worked on a special detail that dealt with runaway kids. They seemed to be genuinely interested in helping me find Sean - if he was on the property they were responsible for patrolling - and took a stack of Sean's photos from me.

The rest of New York City, other than the bus terminals and train stations, was the responsibility of the NYPD. I had called them, but they would not take a report until Sean had been gone for 72 hours. Being from a large Irish-American family in New York, I was able to call several NYPD cops who were distant relatives or family friends and they all reluctantly told me the same thing - serious crime was out of control in the city and realistically, there was nothing the NYPD could do. They offered to take copies of Sean's photo to show their colleagues.

I stayed in New Jersey with my cousins and traveled into the city by train each day to continue my search for Sean. Late in the morning of the third or fourth day, I was still at my cousin's home in New Jersey and talking on the phone with my parents, when the other phone in their home rang and it was Sean. My father told Sean that I was in New York looking for him and Sean told my dad he would meet me on the steps in front of the main branch of the New York Public Library in exactly 35 minutes. Then he added that if I was not there in 35 minutes, he would leave.

I felt sick to my stomach. I did not have a rental car, none of my cousins were home to drive me and the next train to New York wasn't due for two more hours. I called a cab company and asked how long it would take to get me to New York City. The answer was "at least an hour if you're lucky".

I ordered a cab and hung up. Before the cab arrived, I called one of the Port Authority policemen I had recently met with and hurriedly explained the situation and the fact that I was not

23

going to be there within 35 minutes. In desperation, I asked if they still had the photos of Sean and could they send an officer to the library to grab him and hold him until I got there? The officer gently explained that it would not be possible, as the library was too far from any of the train or bus stations they patrolled. I could feel the pain in his voice as he spoke. He had a son close to Sean's age and I sensed that he really wanted to help me, if only he could. I said I understood, then went outside and got into the cab.

I told the driver I needed to be outside the New York Public Library's main branch in 30 minutes and if we made the trip within a half-hour, I would give him a big tip and then we started the mad dash to New York City.

On that cab ride to Manhattan I felt guilt, sadness and anger. We made it to the library in 51 minutes, the cab screeched to a stop in front of the building and I walked quickly towards the massive staircase leading inside. It was lunchtime on a sunny day and the area was packed with tourists and office workers enjoying their lunch hour. My eyes searched frantically for Sean, but I could not see him. I had not made it in time. I had let him down and he had gone back into whatever hellish life he was living in New York.

My heart sank as I got closer to the steps and still did not see my brother. I reached the bottom of the steps and looked up anxiously. Two women, who were standing halfway up the steps, moved away and there he was - sitting on the steps reading a book. My head and heart almost burst. I wanted to kill him, but I also wanted to hug him and apologize for letting him down as his older brother and for failing to protect him.

I walked up the steps towards him quickly and my eyes filled with tears. Tears blurred my vision and I had to stop for a moment to wipe my eyes with my sleeve. When I could see clearly again, my brother was surrounded by several men who were watching my approach. They were the Port Authority police detectives who, in the end, had decided to stake out the library and ensure that Sean did not leave before I got there.

I grabbed Sean and hugged him tightly as I sobbed,

"You little creep! Are you okay?"

One of the plainclothes policemen approached me and asked,

"Are we good here? You all set?"

I thanked him profusely and honestly don't think I have ever been more grateful to anyone in my life.

Letting go of Sean, I took a step away from him. He looked at me, not with the expected expression of overwhelming gratitude and love, but with the familiar bored look of a typical teenager, as he said,

"I suppose you're going to yell at me now?"

After Sean had assured me that he was going to stay with me, we walked away from the library. My head and heart were spinning from the adrenaline. I was very grateful my little brother was alive and with me, but I was also so mad at him I wanted to tear off his head. Most of all, I was absolutely clueless about what I was going to do next.

I decided to rent a car, so Sean and I could spend the next few days driving out to the tip of Long Island to see whatever was there to see. I figured spending some time together would give

Sean the space he needed to share with me the sordid details of his brief stay in New York. It would also give me time to come up with a plan for his future.

However, it turned out that while I was looking for him in the morgue, the runaway shelters and all over the seedy areas around the bus terminal, my poor little brother had not been sleeping on the street, as I had feared. In fact, he had been staying in complete safety in a well-run youth hostel and sleeping each night in a comfortable bed with nice, clean sheets. Moreover, he had been spending his days visiting museums with friendly European college girls he had met at the youth hostel!

Chapter 5

In the end, I ended up going on the media tour in Texas and I took Sean along with me. Southwest Airlines went all out to support our effort for the troops. They were a really special, fun group of people to work with - which was great - because Sean and I definitely needed some lighthearted fun! Looking back, it is noteworthy to me that Sean mentioned that the Southwest folks actually seemed pretty darn happy with their jobs. I told him that I knew from first-hand experience that such obvious job satisfaction was not often experienced by the rest of us in the nation's workforce.

The relaxed and enjoyable nature of our trip to Texas started with the first Southwest flight, when a flight attendant sent a roll of toilet paper rolling down the aisle and challenged passengers to guess the number of squares in the roll in the hope of winning a packet of peanuts. We had done a media event at the airport before leaving, so the flight attendants knew all about our project and asked Sean and I to help pass out the peanuts.

At airport locations throughout Texas, Southwest Airlines created banner size "Christmas cards", addressed to a specific ship or unit, and had them placed in the gate area for passengers and employees to sign and write supportive messages. Local media covered the activities at each airport and local Southwest reps took us to television and radio stations. Southwest even included a story about our soldier support effort in, *Spirit*, their in-flight magazine and many Southwest employees approached

Sean and me to tell us of their own military service or the military service of a loved one.

Another highlight of our time in Texas came in Corpus Christi, where I rented a Mustang convertible sports car and we drove to the Gulf of Mexico. The beaches are beautiful in Corpus Christi and the waters of the Gulf are warm and relaxing. People are permitted to drive their car or truck on the beach, but rental

With Sean at an airport event created by Southwest Airlines

car companies, of course, do not want their shiny, new vehicles getting stuck in the sand.

Therefore, I had been obliged to sign a form on which it was written, in very large print, that I agreed not to drive the rental vehicle on the beach. Of course, Sean and I immediately drove the Mustang down to the Gulf of Mexico and onto the beach! There was a large sign on the beach stating that the sand was groomed for a mile, allowing vehicles to drive that distance without getting stuck. The sign also clearly stated that vehicles venturing beyond the groomed sand were likely to get stuck.

It was late afternoon as Sean and I drove along the water's edge on the empty beach. It was a wonderful, memorable moment. We were both happy and it was great to see Sean's big, bright smile. A fresh salty breeze was blowing and various types of shore birds were flying about and diving into the water.

Even though I graduated from the U.S. Army Infantry School and served in a Ranger unit, I have never been very good at judging distances. Eventually, it occurred to me that we were probably getting pretty close to the end of the section of graded sand and that I would need to turn around soon to avoid getting my expensive car stuck in the sand. Especially since the tide was coming in!

I saw an elderly man walking towards us on the beach and I stopped when we came alongside of him.

"Excuse me, sir", I called out, "where is the end of the graded stretch of sand?"

He smiled and replied,

"Oh, about two miles or so back there" and pointed behind us in the direction we had come from.

Sean and I looked at each other. I had a look of panic and he had a sweet smile of pure delight. I let my foot off the brake pedal and reflexively punched down on the gas. This immediately caused the car to get stuck firmly in the sand. The old man shook his head and said,

"Son, that is going to be a problem."

He was correct - it was a problem! Sean joined the old man behind the rental car and they began pushing. Having grown up in a snowy climate, I had plenty of experience with vehicles stuck in the snow, so I tried the frequently successful strategy of rocking the car out by switching quickly between forward and reverse gear.

The incoming tide of salty Gulf water was already lapping insistently at the left side tires, while the old man and Sean continued to push as hard as they could. At first, the wheels sank further down into the sand and I had a mild panic attack, visualizing the expensive sports car becoming slowly submerged by the incoming tide. Even in the best-case scenario, I would face a huge towing fee just to get the car off the beach.

It seemed to take forever, but I finally managed to rock the car out of the ruts and we began to move slowly forward. I called my thanks to the old man as Sean jumped into the moving car and I made sure to stay in motion on the firm, wet sand.

During our time together in Texas, Sean and I discussed the situation at home until he concluded that there was nothing he could do to fix things and he had no choice but to stick it out until he graduated from high school.

Sean and I spending Christmas in Germany with the U.S. Army's 2ⁿᵈ ACR.
This was Sean's first exposure to soldiering in Europe.

Chapter 6

When Sean was still in high school, I took him with me to spend Christmas in Germany, where I went to distribute Christmas mail to U.S. troops. This Christmas was very special for us, because the Army unit that Sean and I visited, the elite 2nd Armored Cavalry Regiment (2nd ACR), had been 'adopted' by a nationally televised show.

I appeared on the show with Dear Abby and we both encouraged viewers to send lots of cards and letters to the 'adopted' unit for Christmas. The television show also arranged for Olympic Gold Medal winner, Bruce Jenner, to fly to Germany and further boost morale by helping me give out the unit's special Christmas mail.

The unit was stationed along the Iron Curtain, which it patrolled 24 hours a day. Sean and I were able to spend one night sleeping on bunks in the junior officers' barracks. Sean spent hours speaking with the young Lieutenants, who weren't much older than he was at that time. They told Sean riveting stories about their travel all over Europe and the great responsibility the Army gave them as young leaders.

That Christmas and New Year was also memorable because the Berlin Wall had just been torn down and the people of East Germany were free for the first time since the end of WWII. Sean and I went to Berlin for New Year's Eve and it was an amazing experience to watch a New Year filled with freedom arrive in the middle of the huge crowds at the Brandenburg Gate.

Chapter 7

ENLISTED MEDIC AND JUMP WINGS

Time passed and Sean finished high school – despite having to endure the difficult situation at home. Looking back, I can see that medicine was Sean's vocation from an early age, as even before graduating high school, he had already become a valued volunteer worker at a nearby hospital and was getting exposure to emergency medicine.

Although Sean had been accepted by Michigan State University, he decided to put off college for a year and enlist as a medic in a hospital unit in the Army Reserve. I was very proud to attend his graduation from medic training at Ft. Sam Houston in San Antonio, Texas. 'Ft. Sam' is the home of Army medicine and a place that would play a big part in Sean's future.

After Sean's graduation ceremony, I noticed many photos of soldiers lining the walls of the auditorium. When I asked Sean about the photos he replied,

"Those are dead medics who won the Medal of Honor. Our sergeants made sure we understood they were heroes, but they ended up as dead medics and dead medics can't save the lives of any more soldiers."

After the graduation ceremony we had dinner along the famous River Walk in downtown San Antonio. Like most visitors to the city, Sean loved San Antonio and later on in his career, as a PA student at Ft. Sam Houston, he lived near River Walk.

Upon completion of his initial Army training, Sean returned home and began college. At that point in his life, he had already decided he loved medicine and intended to study biology as an undergraduate and then go to med school to become a doctor. However, his interest in serving as an Army officer overseas continued while he attended monthly training with his Army Reserve hospital unit.

Sean was a great soldier in the Army Reserve. He quickly earned the respect of his unit's leadership, which included physicians and Registered Nurses. One of the officers, a Registered Nurse who worked in a high volume emergency room in Detroit, suggested that Sean change his college major from biology to study nursing instead. She explained.

"Getting a four year nursing degree will be great preparation for medical school and if you change your mind about becoming a doctor, you will always have a job waiting for you in nursing, anywhere in the U.S."

Sean took her advice and was accepted into the very competitive nursing program at Michigan State University. He later told me,

"Studying Nursing at Michigan State was the smartest thing I could have done".

He also joined the Army ROTC program with the goal of becoming an officer and serving in Europe. Sean excelled in ROTC, since he was already an enlisted soldier, and went to training at Ft. Lewis in Washington State and Tripler Army Hospital in Honolulu. In his senior year he was the cadet responsible for supervising the daily exercise program at 6 a.m.

Between his junior and senior year in college, Sean was selected by the ROTC program to attend the very challenging three-week U.S. Army Airborne course, at Ft. Benning, GA. I remember that Sean was very excited about this great opportunity to earn the silver wings of a paratrooper.

The three weeks of Airborne school were divided into the physically grueling Ground Week, Tower Week and Jump Week when the students tested their two weeks of training by actually jumping out of perfectly good airplanes. The norm for Airborne classes is to do five jumps over the course of Jump Week. The graduation ceremony is held on the 'drop zone', after the 5th parachute jump and family members are invited to view the final jump and graduation ceremony from bleachers.

After each parachute landing, during Jump Week the students gather up their parachutes, get into formation and run off the drop zone. This allows the instructors to inspect the students and discover any indications of injury, because when students are so close to finishing the course, there is a tremendous incentive for them to hide injuries.

Airborne School is known to be one of the Army's toughest training programs, with a very high failure rate. Most of the students who fail to complete the course drop out owing to the heavy routine of constant push-ups, running and other very taxing exercises. Injuries are the other major challenge to completing the course and the sight of young soldiers hobbling on crutches around the barracks and mess halls of the school complex is very common.

If an Airborne student's injuries are too severe, they are dropped from the course and have to start again at the beginning - they are "recycled." This frightening possibility leads most

Airborne students to dread even the sight of a hobbled comrade. Students will even cross the street to avoid the path of an ex-Airborne student in a cast or on crutches. Some injured students pass their recuperation time working as a sort of receptionist on the ground floor entrance to a barracks. They sit at their post with their crutches beside them while able-bodied students pass by with their eyes averted.

Sean and I had worked out a plan. I would fly to Ft. Benning to see him make his final jump and then I would pin the silver parachutist badge, known as 'jump wings', on his chest. After that, we planned to drive to the Florida panhandle for some brotherly fun.

Sean and I had spoken by phone on the Sunday before Jump Week, when he would be making his first parachute jump. I remember hearing the excitement in his voice - he could hardly believe he was so near to achieving this major step forward in his career. The first two weeks had been grueling and as a ROTC cadet and Army Reservist, Sean had faced an extra-tough challenge to exercise and work harder than the average Airborne student.

Those students on the course who were commissioned officers or officer cadets, from ROTC and West Point, were subject to extra harassment (extra 'care and motivation') and given extra push-ups and exercises by the sergeants who ran the course. Sean took it in his stride and, as a former enlisted soldier, actually enjoyed the fact that the officers and officer cadets were getting messed with by the enlisted sergeant instructors.

Late afternoon, on the Monday of Sean's Jump Week, I received a panicked message to call my mom because something had happened to Sean at Airborne School. Two thoughts immediately came to mind: 1) stories of Airborne students being paralyzed by injuries and 2) fate must have a strong reason to stop men of the Grimes' family from graduating from Airborne school. Years earlier, as a young soldier in Airborne school, I had injured my shoulder and was not able to graduate.

I spoke with our mom who gave me a phone number for Ft. Benning - which I quickly called. The sergeant who answered said that Cadet Grimes was right next to him and then I heard Sean's voice saying,

"This is Cadet Grimes". Then realizing he was speaking to me, Sean simply said, "I broke my ankle on my first jump. I tried to run off the drop zone but I couldn't".

"How bizarre!" I thought after ending my call with Sean – "It seems that fate just doesn't want Grimes' men to be paratroopers."

I caught the next flight to Atlanta and drove to Ft. Benning to pick up Sean and then go to the Florida panhandle as planned. Sean was waiting by the front door of his barracks, sitting forlornly with his crutches and duffel bag. Healthy Airborne students were going in and out of the barracks and without exception, each healthy student made sure they did not make eye contact with Sean, or me. No one wanted to see an example of the sad fate that might await them if they landed badly on their parachute jump the next day.

It was a joyless dinner for us that night in a restaurant crowded with happy families. The waitress came to our table, saw Sean's solemn face and then his bandaged ankle and crutches. She shook her head slowly and spoke in a soft, kind voice,

"Oh darlin', did you break yourself on a jump?"

If an Airborne student sustains an injury during Jump Week, it is still possible for them to earn their paratrooper wings after they have recovered. Injured soldiers who are able to return to the Airborne course within six months, can simply resume making parachute jumps until they reach the required minimum of four. If the student does not return to make the remaining jumps within six months of their injury, they are required to re-take the entire, grueling course.

After our trip to Florida, Sean returned to Michigan State and the ROTC unit, assuming it would be easy to obtain orders to send him back to Airborne school as soon as possible to earn his 'wings'. Unfortunately, it was not meant to be. The six-month time limit passed and Sean still had not received orders to return to Airborne. This was a tough time for Sean who had set his heart on being a paratrooper.

However, when the next summer rolled around and ROTC offered him another set of orders for Airborne school – he grabbed the opportunity with both hands! Off he went, back to Ft. Benning, where he repeated the full, arduous Airborne training. And this time, he managed to avoid injury, complete the jumps and finally, earn his silver paratrooper wings!

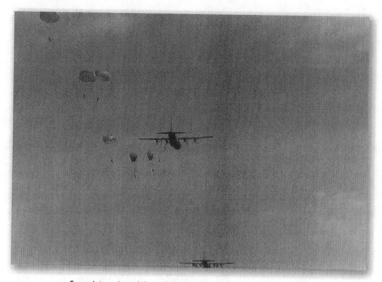

Second time through Jump School is the charm! Sean gets his wings.

Great day for the Grimes family at Michigan State University! Sean graduates with a Degree in Nursing and is commissioned as an officer in the U.S. Army.

Chapter 8

If someone had asked me, before March 4th 2005, what had been the proudest moment in my life; I would have described a day back in 1997. It was the day Sean graduated with a Nursing Degree from Michigan State University and, just a few hours later, received his commission as a Second Lieutenant in the U.S. Army.

After Sean's four years of hard work, participation and leadership in the Army ROTC program, I was full of pride for his high achievements as I pinned the gold lieutenant's bar on his uniform - moments after he had been sworn in as a U.S. Army officer. The whole family shared my pride and many aunts and uncles had flown in from New York and New Jersey to attend Sean's graduation and commissioning.

After the last ceremony of the day, we all gathered at a good restaurant to continue celebrating Sean's achievements over dinner. It was a very sweet moment for me to stand in front of our assembled family, speaking words of praise and honor for my brother and then leading all of our family in a toast for him and his bright future. He sat with his million-dollar smile and absolutely radiated happiness. He might almost have been as happy and proud of himself, as I was of my beloved kid brother!

Sean asked to be stationed in Germany and was assigned to the large Army hospital in the city of Langsthul.

Sean (far right) supervising the unloading of a casualty from a Medevac helicopter in Kosovo

Chapter 9

DUTY IN GERMANY AND KOSOVO U.N. PEACEKEEPING

Serving as an Army officer in Germany was something Sean had always wanted to do, ever since he had visited Germany with me and spent time with the 2nd Armored Cavalry Regiment. Peacetime duty in Germany was ideal for a single, young officer who loved to travel. There were plenty of other young officers who wanted to explore Germany and the rest of Europe. I remember that Sean especially loved Paris.

A special highlight of Sean's tour in Germany, was being deployed to Kosovo as part of the United Nations peacekeeping operation. His time in Kosovo found him working as an emergency room nurse in the Army's last M.A.S.H. unit. He also went out into civilian communities, with infantry patrols, to provide vital medical care to civilians. These medical forays into the ancient towns allowed Sean to combine his love of providing much needed medical care, with the satisfaction of being in the field with combat troops.

Sean had a special place in his heart for kids. In Kosovo, the U.S. Army hospital provided care for the local civilian population giving Sean the opportunity to treat their kids.

One day, an infant was brought to the front gate of the M.A.S.H. unit. The baby had been found on a roadside and the U.S. Army nurses had named her 'April'. Sean made a command decision and put himself in charge of organizing the duty roster for diaper changing. Throughout the time that baby April was

Sean feeding a toddler brought to the U.S. Army M.A.S.H. hospital in Kosovo

a patient in the Army's care, Sean made it his business to track down and remind the next medical professional in line to change a diaper as needed!

Sean ended his tour of duty in Germany working as the nurse in charge of a shift in the emergency room and with a promotion to the rank of Captain.

I went to Germany to visit Sean before his tour of duty was over. He was supposed to meet me in the arrival area of the Frankfurt Airport and I was waiting for him in the baggage area. Suddenly, I was tackled from behind and knocked to the ground.

Sean holding baby 'April' at the 212th M.A.S.H. unit in Kosovo

My eyes closed as I fell, feeling the weight of a man's heavy body taking me down.

When I opened my eyes, I was staring into Sean's smiling face – he was my assailant!

"Hey, big brother!" he said joyfully, as he got up and then helped me to my feet.

I could barely recognize him! The tall, thin, good-looking college kid had turned into a confident, handsome and powerful man. He had grown a few inches since I last saw him and added at least twenty pounds of hard muscle.

Sean had become just like the cosmopolitan, young Army officers and sergeants he had met years before. In the last 3 ½ years, he had traveled all over Europe with his fellow officers.

He lived in a civilian apartment in the local German town and shopped in the local markets, speaking to the stall-owners in German. As was his tradition, he still liked to spend New Year's Eve in a beautiful city with a pretty girl - except now the city was Paris, instead of New York!

Sean took me to the base hospital and showed me where he worked in the Emergency Room. It was clear that both the soldiers he worked with and those for whom he provided medical care, liked and respected him as a medical provider and officer.

Sean and I made two side trips while I was visiting him. Our first trip was to the beautiful Polish city of Krakow and from there, we took a northbound train along the entire length of the country to the port city of Gdansk. Gdansk was the hometown of Lech Walesa and the Solidarity movement, whose brave determination closed the last chapter on the brutal communist domination of Eastern Europe.

The train ride from Krakow to Gdansk was the longest time Sean and I had really talked since our road trip, after he ran away from home, years earlier. Obviously, I knew of Sean's success as an Army officer and Registered Nurse, but it was different actually having hours to really get to know him again as a confident adult. He was amazing. I was so proud of him and more than a little envious of his firm sense of direction for his life and career. Moreover, he had found an organization that would give him all the training, responsibility, professional growth and adventure he wanted. On that train ride, I began the process of changing my mental image of Sean, from a "little brother" who needed my protection, to that of a capable man and friend. It was wonderful to find that he had become a confident man, whom I could relate to and enjoy as a peer. Sean was far more capable and secure in himself than I was at his age!

After returning to Germany from our trip to Poland, we rested a few days before driving to Paris. It was my first trip to Paris and Sean was in his element as my tour guide, introducing me to Paris in the same way I had introduced him to New York City, years before. Sean spoke passible French and he showed me all the memorable sights.

Each night, we would go back to the hotel after a great dinner and I would go to bed like the old married guy I was. Sean would shower, put on clean clothes and head back out into the night and when I awoke the next morning, he would be snoring loudly in the next bed.

On our last morning in Paris, I woke up to see Sean's bed was empty and had not been slept in. My mind immediately went into negative hyper-drive, feeding me stories of American military men who had been killed, kidnapped by terrorists or injured by robbers. My heart raced as I tried to think of what I should do and whom I should call. After a few panicked moments, a clear and calming thought came to me: Sean was an American military officer, so the process of finding him would be the responsibility of the U.S. government, beginning with the U.S. Embassy in Paris. I got up and began to get dressed and then I heard a key being inserted into our hotel room door. The door opened and in walked a very tired, but very happy-looking, Sean.

Shortly after heading out the night before, Sean had met a group of young college women from the University of Texas who were visiting Paris for the first time. As an American Army officer, and a gentleman, he had felt it his duty to take this group of attractive young Texans all over Paris. Until the sun began to rise and the young women no longer had the energy to stay awake.

Chapter 10

Sean's duty in Kosovo reinforced his love for emergency medicine and his desire to be in the field with front line troops. The problem for Sean was that Army nurses did not go into direct combat and instead, provided care in field hospitals set close to the field of battle.

However, the Army *did* have a career opportunity that would allow Sean the chance to combine emergency medicine and direct duty on the battlefield: he could apply to become a Physician Assistant (PA) and attend the Physician Assistant course run by the Department of Defense.

The U.S. Army has been a world leader, since WW II, in the development and advancement of trauma care. One of the Army's latest advances in battlefield medicine at that time, was the deployment of Physician Assistants to the field aid stations that were part of combat units. The PA's provided American soldiers with the fastest access to high-level medical care available in any military in the world.

Applying for the PA program presented Sean with two profound career dilemmas. He had recently been promoted to Captain and was highly respected in the Army nursing community. He consistently received the highest possible rating in his annual officer evaluations and was on the fast track in his current career field.

However, if he applied to become a Physician Assistant, it would effectively signal that he wanted to work outside of nursing. If he applied for the PA program, but was not selected, he would leave the Army and use his GI Bill education benefits to go to medical school and become a physician.

The other challenge was that Sean had already been promoted from 1st Lieutenant to Captain and students on the PA course could not have a rank higher than 1st Lieutenant. This meant that Sean would have to ask to be demoted to 1st Lieutenant - a move that is virtually unheard of in the U.S. military - considering how hard soldiers have to work to receive promotion - and even more unusual for officers!

However, Sean wanted to serve with soldiers in the field, so he needed to become a Physician Assistant. He applied for the PA program and agreed to be demoted and I was amazed that he was willing to go backwards in rank. Most of his fellow officers thought he was crazy and did not hesitate to tell him so!

Happily, Sean was selected for PA school. He packed up his belongings in Germany and said sad goodbyes to the soldiers and officers he loved and with whom he had served. His 3 ½ years as an Army officer in Germany had been even better than he had hoped for. He was off to Ft. Sam Houston and an apartment close to the famous River Walk.

Even with his nursing degree and years of medical experience, Sean still found the PA course very demanding. For the first time in almost four years, he had to study and study hard to survive. The military Physician Assistant program is a very challenging two year program, one year of intense classes followed by a year of clinical training. However, staying true to his unselfish character Sean went out of his way to help fellow students with their studies.

Most of us seem to enjoy staying where we are career-wise, we hit a plateau and become comfortable. Looking back, I really admire the fact that Sean was willing to leave his comfort zone as a successful and respected Registered Nurse and put himself through a very high-pressure, academic course.

After finishing his academic program at Ft. Sam Houston in San Antonio, Sean was sent for clinical training at Madigan Army Medical center at Ft. Campbell, KY. Ft. Campbell is home to the celebrated, 'Screaming Eagles', of the 101st Airborne Division and Sean did rotations through the various medical specialties in the hospital. His favorite rotations were in the Emergency Room and Obstetrics and Sean delivered quite a few babies while at Ft. Campbell.

Sean told me of one especially meaningful episode while at Ft. Campbell. He was in his General Medicine rotation and a young female soldier came in with the flu. Sean noticed she had a very noticeable, but also very treatable, skin growth on her face. It was the sort of thing that would have caused considerable teasing and ridicule throughout her childhood. Sean asked the young soldier why it had not been taken care of before and she replied that her parents had not had the money or interest to get the skin condition fixed. Sean had told her,

"Well, Army medicine can fix that now." and gone off to find the duty surgeon to arrange a consultation for the soldier.

Shortly thereafter, the soldier had the surgery that fixed her face and Sean later told me that it had been, "a day when I was very proud to be a solider". After hearing his story, I thought, "This is a day when I am damn proud of my brother *and* the Army".

Once Sean had been accepted to the Physician Assistant course, he had quickly volunteered to be assigned to Korea after graduation. He had never been to Asia and wanted to see it. He mentioned that volunteering for Korea, after he had earlier volunteered for Germany, meant he would be able to have his pick of his next assignments. He thought that Ft. Carson, Colorado, would be his choice when he finally got a chance to live in the U.S. for an extended period of time.

When the terrorist attacks happened on 9/11, Sean and his PA classmates watched in horror and disbelief as the Twin Towers of the World Trade Center collapsed. The Port Authority of New York and New Jersey ran the World Trade Center and a total of 37 Port Authority police officers died in the Twin Towers that day, as they worked to rescue the trapped and injured. Sean and I both wondered if any of the police officers who had helped us years earlier, when Sean had run away from home, were included in the Port Authority death toll that day.

Sean wanted to go to Iraq right away, but he was sent to Korea. Before shipping out to Korea, however, he volunteered for Flight Surgeon school, where he learned to meet the unique medical needs of Army pilots and for this, Sean was awarded his Flight Surgeon wings. He also attended the Army's tough Air Assault course and was awarded his Air Assault wings upon graduation.

Chapter 11

PHYSICIAN ASSISTANT IN SOUTH KOREA

In South Korea, duty for the U.S. Army was very intense, probably the most intense in the peacetime Army. South Korea and North Korea were still technically at war, as the Korean War was merely paused by a truce and not actually ended. U.S. forces were stationed along the De-militarized Zone (DMZ), on the border between peaceful and prosperous South Korea and poverty ridden and militarily powerful North Korea.

Sean worked hard in Korea and as the unit Physician Assistant for the 6th Battalion, 37th Field Artillery Regiment, he was required to undertake two jobs. He provided medical care for soldiers and performed the staff and leaderships duties of the Unit Medical Officer. He also supervised the Troop Medical Clinic (TMC).

Whilst looking over Sean's personnel papers, I found one of his Officer Evaluation Reports from his time in Korea. In the report, a senior officer describes how Sean was initially responsible for the medical care of the 450 U.S. soldiers in his unit, as well as the 3,000 other U.S. troops and family members who used the TMC under his supervision.

In addition, Sean's supervisor noted that Sean had volunteered to have another 650 patients assigned to him for primary care. Moreover, since Sean's arrival, the medical readiness statistics for the medical unit he led had improved to the point at which their readiness was the highest of all the Artillery units in Korea!

The report also describes how Sean devised an innovative plan to resolve staffing shortages at the Troop Medical Clinic. Sean organized a rotation of his medics from various line units into the main clinic. This plan gave the under-utilized unit medics more first hand medical experience - whilst improving TMC patient access at the same time.

Finally, the senior officer described Sean as the, "*most conscientious provider I have worked with in my 16 years of service*". He also noted that Sean had volunteered to teach English to Koreans *and* volunteered to provide medical coverage to local sporting events. The report mentioned that Sean had volunteered for duty in Iraq and that he had saved the lives of, at least, three U.S. soldiers in Korea. The evaluation ends,

"*I would trust the care of my men and my family to 'Doc' Grimes. Of course, I want this soldier with me in combat.*"

In his scarce free time, Sean would join the other young officers on visits to Seoul and it was there that he met the lovely, young woman he hoped would become his wife, Leah Anne.

Chapter 12

The last day of pre-Iraq leave finally came. Sean had spent his leave at my home in southern California and now it was time to go to war. It was a surreal experience for me to be driving Sean to Los Angeles International Airport. We were mostly silent on the drive and when we did speak, it was mostly of his expectation of returning from duty in Iraq to be stationed at Ft. Carson. I had already spoken with my wife of selling our home in California and also heading to Colorado Springs. We would enjoy a dramatic decrease in the cost of living, a pleasant change of scenery and most of all, have the enjoyment of being near Sean and Leah Anne when they began their own family. My wife and I love kids and were looking forward very much to helping Sean and Leah Anne as new parents.

Sean and I arrived at the airport terminal from which his charter flight was scheduled to depart. I pulled over to the curb, hit the trunk-release button and stood next to Sean as he pulled his duffel bag out of the trunk. I noticed other young men with short hair being dropped off - some by older people, probably parents and others by young women holding back their tears - or stepping out of taxicabs, alone.

I had always wondered what it was like for the fathers who, during the Viet Nam war, drove their soldier sons to the airport to fly off into harm's way. Now, I knew how those fathers felt. I realized that Sean was going to a place where US troops were killed or wounded on a daily basis. However,

I told myself to stay calm, because I believed Sean would spend his tour of duty as a Physician Assistant, in the relative safety of a base camp hospital.

I hugged Sean tightly and told him I loved him and that I was very, very proud of him. He walked away from me towards the other soldiers and I thought of the other people dropping off soldiers, who also had jobs that would take them into danger each day. Some of these soldiers would be returning home to their families in gleaming silver caskets. These soldiers could be giving their family or friends their last hug, last handshake, last smile and final wave.

I thanked God that my little brother was going to spend his tour of duty in a base camp medical facility. I knew that Sean was going to see and treat soldiers with ghastly injuries and would have to deal with the emotional impact of those sights and experiences. I had already decided to ask our uncle, who saw combat in Viet Nam, to speak privately with Sean when he came home on leave – as one combat veteran to another. I thanked God over and over that Sean was a PA and would be reasonably safe in Iraq.

The sign at the entrance to Sean's base camp in Iraq

Chapter 13

THE BATTLEFIELD

The plan was for Sean's unit to fly first to Kuwait and then convoy into Iraq. Communication with Sean was an occasional email and an even more infrequent phone call. I knew he was very busy because, as usual, he was filling two roles as an officer - providing care as the unit's Physician Assistant *and* managing a large group of medics who had been assigned to support the various units and platoons. Furthermore, Sean was also responsible for the medics who staffed a forward aid station, which was an ambulance located outside of the base camp and closer to the battlefield.

We received word from Sean that his unit was heading out to Iraq and we would not be getting any emails until they had settled into their base camp. After Sean's unit moved into Iraq, I cringed every time the news came on and announced the latest casualties in Iraq. I thought of the parents or the spouse of each soldier or Marine who had been wounded or killed. The closest family member would hear their doorbell ring and open the front door to be confronted by two military officers, looking very sad and uncomfortable. The higher-ranking officer would speak first asking, "Can we come in, please?" And then they would deliver their heartbreaking news.

Every couple of weeks, I would get a call from Sean. My cell phone would ring and the caller ID would show something strange and unknown. Sean's calls were, by necessity, short and the tone of his voice changed as his unit quickly began to take casualties.

Soldiers he had known from his time in Korea, as well as those he did not know, were being killed and seriously wounded.

Sean was not only a great medical provider, he was also a great soldier. He attended to the details of soldiering and insisted on doing things the right way. He was responsible for the Forward Aid Station located outside of the base camp walls and closer to the battlefield. When he and his unit had rotated into the area, Sean noticed that the Forward Aid Station had been placed beside a major road, making it a great terrorist target. To remedy this, Sean ordered his troops to increase the fortifications around the Forward Aid Station. The troops grumbled at the extra work, but Sean made sure it was done and the work paid off in 'saved lives' weeks later, when a terrorist detonated a car filled with explosives near the Forward Aid Station. The terrorist was

Sean riding in an armored ambulance in Iraq - the large patch on his left shoulder is the unit insignia for the 2nd Infantry Division.

vaporized, but no harm came to the medics behind the increased shielding that Sean had insisted on.

Unfortunately, not every soldier rises to the demands of wartime duty and occasionally, Sean had to be 'the hammer' and discipline troops who were not doing their job. Sean lived by the Army's Leadership Credo of, "Hard right instead of easy wrong", because *real leaders* always do the right thing - no matter how hard or unpopular - instead of the quicker, easier but *wrong* thing to do.

One frequent topic of our phone calls and emails was Sean's rotation back to the U.S., after his tour in Iraq was completed. Instead of going back to Korea, it had been decided that Sean's

Sean (L) with Scout Platoon Leader (C) and one his Medic Sergeants (R)
after meeting with local sheik to discuss setting up a medical clinic for Iraqi women and children.

entire contingent of 2nd Infantry soldiers would rotate to Ft. Carson, in Colorado Springs, one of the most beautiful spots in America. Sean's unit had Internet access and he used some of his limited free time to check out online real estate listings for Colorado Springs. It would have been funny to eavesdrop on some of my calls with Sean. Even as he was dodging bullets and bombs in Iraq, we were having earnest discussions about the relative merits of a variety of real estate listings in Colorado Springs – especially 3-bedroom versus 4-bedroom homes.

Sean also expressed to me his concern about the future awaiting the most seriously wounded troops, after their return to the U.S. More soldiers were surviving their injuries in Iraq but, unfortunately, they were losing arms and legs in the process.

Sean was ready to come back to the U.S. after serving in Europe, Korea and now Iraq. He was ready to enjoy some conventional living with the women who would be his new wife. I was really enjoying having Sean as a brother instead of viewing him as my 'first son'. He was an awesome guy and we had so much fun together. He was great with my son and would be an excellent dad to his own kids. My wife and I were already looking forward to being aunt and uncle to the kids Sean would one day raise.

Chapter 14

As the day grew warmer on March 4th the vehicles of the Scout Platoon patrol continued their search for the signs of terrorist networks driving down a dirt road on the east side of Tammim, a village in the suburbs of Ar Ramadi. Sean's vehicle, the command vehicle with the call sign "HQ24U', was the last Humvee in the patrol and was easily identifiable as the command vehicle, by the unique communication gear on its back.

As the patrol vehicles were crossing over a canal of the Euphrates River, a group of Iraqi men was standing in a decrepit industrial building - watching. These were the men who had been carrying shovels in the pre-dawn darkness. The large bullet-shaped item they had been carrying was a powerful artillery shell. These terrorists had buried the artillery shell beneath the dirt road on which the Scout patrol was now driving and were waiting for the last Humvee to pass over the bomb - before detonating it. When HQ24U was over the bomb a massive explosion shook the ground.

Chapter 15

On Friday, March 4th, 2005 at 1:50 pm, I was waiting to begin a presentation at a law firm, when I noticed I had a voicemail message on my cell phone. As I still had a little time left before my appointment, I checked my message. I heard my mother's voice telling me to call her right away because she had some bad news. I immediately thought of elderly relatives who were in failing health and wondered which one had died. At no time did it even enter my mind that something could have happened to Sean - it was simply not possible.

I called my mother, who picked up on the first ring and just said,

"The Army's here. Sean was killed".

Six words - that in an instant changed my life and broke my heart. I stuttered into the phone,

"Are you sure? How can that be?"

A male voice came onto the phone and introduced himself as a Lieutenant Colonel before saying,

"I am very sorry for your loss. Captain Grimes was killed today in Anbar province. While on patrol, an Improvised Explosive Device detonated, destroying his Humvee. To the best of our knowledge, he died almost instantly. Again, sir, I am so very sorry for your loss".

I dropped the phone and looked up at the room full of people who were looking at me strangely. I said,

"I just found out my boy was killed today in Iraq. I have to go home now and tell my wife".

The women in the room began to cry as I packed up my briefcase and headed, dazed, to my car. I called my wife on her cell. She was in line in the grocery store.

"Sean's dead. I just spoke to my mom and an Army officer. I'm going to come home now".

The next few days are a blur as I just lay around weeping uncontrollably. Sean's body was flown from Iraq to the Army hospital in Langsthul, the place Sean where had spent 3 ½ happy years at the start of his Army career, and then on to Dover Air Force Base in Maryland.

Sean had asked me to be the executor of his will, so somehow I had to pull myself together to fly to New Jersey and arrange for his funeral and burial. Sean wanted to be buried out on Long Island in the same cemetery as our grandparents. I went to Newark Airport to meet Leah Anne's flight and my family actually ended up getting together for Sean in New Jersey - but not for the reason we had planned.

Sean's will stated that he wanted a closed casket funeral and wake and the time inevitably came to take Sean's coffin from the funeral home to the church. However, once all of the mourners had left the room, I had the funeral director open the coffin. Sean was in a dress uniform with all his ribbons and awards: paratrooper wings, air assault wings, flight surgeon wings and his Combat Medic badge. The military morticians did a great job on

Sean. He looked just like my beloved, handsome little brother. It seemed as if he was merely taking a nap.

I patted his hand and told him I loved him and that I was so very, very proud of him. Then I reached into my coat pocket and took out a family photo I loved, showing Sean at my house just before he had left for Iraq. Sean was in uniform, with his beaming smile and holding my son Scott, as I stood proudly next to him. I placed the photo gently on Sean's chest over his heart and leaned over to kiss his forehead softly, just like I did when he was a sleeping toddler, and said, "I love you, my little Sean." I then told the funeral director to close the coffin.

Chapter 16

After the funeral service was over, we faced a 90-mile drive in heavy traffic from New Jersey to the cemetery in Long Island. It had been arranged by U.S. Senator Frank Lautenberg that a police car would escort the funeral cortege all the way across the New Jersey state line into New York State.

As we walked out of the church following Sean's casket, I caught sight of the police escort vehicle at the head of the long line of parked cars. And it stopped me in my tracks. The police car in the lead was from the Port Authority police and two Port Authority policemen had joined the local police officers outside the church. Then all the assembled police officers and military personnel snapped to attention and saluted, as Sean's coffin passed them on the way to the hearse.

After days of non-stop sobbing, I had managed to remain stone-faced during the church service. I stayed that way until the funeral procession entered the approach to the George Washington Bridge. At the entrance to the bridge, the Port Authority police car in front slowed down, causing all the following cars to slow. I looked out the car window for the cause of the slowdown and saw a line of Port Authority police officers saluting as Sean's body passed by.

I thought back to the day when Sean was a young runaway and the Port Authority detectives had gone to the public library to watch over him until I arrived. I though of the hundreds of police officers, firefighters and paramedics killed in the line of duty on 9/11 as they worked to rescue the trapped and wounded in the Twin Towers. My brother had been killed avenging those attacks and now, years later, the Port Authority police were again watching over my beloved little brother. Emotion overwhelmed me and I began to cry.

Chapter 17

SERIOUS PEOPLE CAN STILL ENJOY LIFE!

Too often in life, people believe that being focused and successful means you are not supposed to have fun. Sean was highly focused on his life goals and committed to excellence - as an officer and as a medical provider - but he was also a compassionate and fun loving guy. Sean always looked for joy in his life and created it for himself and those around him. Sean traveled all over the world where he enjoyed the company of fun and interesting people.

Sean's nursing program at Michigan State was very demanding and so was his leadership position in ROTC, but he also found time to enjoy being a member of the Kappa Sigma fraternity. He had a lot of fun in the company of his Kappa Sigma brothers when college was in session and often spent Spring Break in Florida, with some of his Kappa Sigma family.

I never knew this about my brother - but he was also a proud 'Deadhead'. Whenever he had the chance, he would stop shaving, put on a tie-dyed shirt and follow the Grateful Dead.

In looking over Sean's Officer Evaluations, I found more examples of Sean's ability to weave fun into his work in a mention by senior officers of Sean's commitment to the physical fitness of his unit in Germany. He had taken the initiative to organize a new flag football league for hospital staff – managing to increase fitness and boost morale at the same time. He also received praise for organizing trips to Paris and Munich, for the

ROTC cadets who were spending their summer training at his Army hospital in Germany. I know the ROTC cadets who went to Paris and Munich with Sean had a great time and heard much from Sean about how fun and rewarding Army service in Europe could be.

Chapter 18

COMPASSION AND LOYALTY

After Sean's death, I heard many stories about him that reflected his selfless personality and deep compassion for others. One story came from a young woman who had been one

of Sean's dearest friends. I met her the day Sean graduated from Michigan State University and received his commission as an officer in the U.S. Army. When she and Sean first met, he was 16 and she was 21 and waitressing at the Big Boy restaurant in our hometown, where Sean had his first ever part time job, working as the host. The first time Sean spoke to her he said,

'Did you know there are only two people in the world who know the recipe for the Big Boy sauce and that they can never fly in the same plane at the same time?'

His friend continued: "*Sean was mature beyond his years, so despite our age difference, we became fast friends. Sean was simply one of the smartest, most thoughtful, kindest, funniest people I have ever known. After I was diagnosed with cancer, Sean came with me on the day I had my first chemo treatment. When all my hair fell out, he told me I still looked beautiful. I was with him on the day he became a lieutenant and he stood next to me on the day I graduated from medical school (cheering the loudest of anyone, including my own family!) The last time I saw Sean was when he was living in Germany, but we lost touch after that. I am so proud of all that Sean accomplished in such a short time on this earth and I am grateful that I was blessed to have known him. And, just as I have over years past, I will think of him often and for always.*"

My wife, son and I attended various memorial services for the soldiers of the 2nd Infantry Division who were killed in Iraq and, on many occasions, the eulogies were given by wounded soldiers who had fought alongside the fallen soldier. I was only to learn later, that many of those wounded troops giving eulogies had first been treated in combat by Sean.

Outside the main gate to Ft Carson, in view of Pike's Peak, is a memorial on which the names of the soldiers assigned to

Ft. Carson, who were later killed in Iraq and Afghanistan, are etched in granite. After Sean's unit had left Iraq and returned to Ft Carson, there was a memorial service at which the names of the soldiers killed in the deployment were unveiled. After the ceremony, I noticed a small group of soldiers looking at the place where Sean's name was inscribed. The soldiers were taking turns to touch Sean's name on the cold granite.

I approached the soldiers, introduced myself and asked how they knew Sean. They were medics assigned to 'Charlie Med', the field hospital on Sean's base camp. Through their tears, they told me they had worked with Sean in the emergency room at Charlie Med, when he was not on patrol or doing other duties. These young medics were actually on duty when the bomb exploded under Sean's Humvee. They had worked hard to revive him, desperate to save his life. One of the medics had been the person who had manually pumped air into Sean's lungs in the emergency room. They told me that Sean was quick to share his knowledge and had repeatedly told them that once their tour of duty in the Army ended, he expected them to use their educational benefits to study nursing.

At another memorial service, an enlisted soldier told me that a few months into their deployment in Iraq, he had approached Sean and asked for his advice. He said he had been hesitant to bother Sean, who was a Captain and a very busy officer. However, this soldier told me that Sean had been delighted that the soldier had asked for his help. The soldier explained that one his children back in the U.S. had been suffering a health condition that their local physician could not fix. Sean had called the soldier's wife in the U.S. to hear firsthand what was going on with the child. Then he had figured out what the condition actually was and called

77

the child's physician to share this important information. The doctor had concurred with Sean's long distance diagnosis and the soldier's sick child was then able to get the correct treatment!

While at a memorial for Sean in San Antonio, a classmate from his Physician Assistant program class told me a story from Sean's time living in downtown San Antonio. There had been a homeless man living near Sean's apartment, who saw Sean in his Army uniform one day and told him that he had once been a soldier, too. Sean questioned him about his time in the Army and determined that the man had, indeed, been a soldier. Sean would not give him money for alcohol, but he did help the man during the entire time he lived in San Antonio. Sean regularly provided him with food and vitamins and let him shower in his apartment and wash his clothes there as well.

My hometown of Mission Viejo, CA is a few miles north of the large U.S. Marine Corps base at Camp Pendleton. Our town has 'adopted' a Marine unit at Camp Pendleton and the unit regularly attends some of our local events. It was at a community car wash that I met a group of Marines who had been stationed alongside Sean in Iraq - after I had introduced my son and myself to the group.

After hearing our last name, one of the senior Marine sergeants asked if by any chance we were related to a great soldier he had met in Iraq, by the name of Captain Grimes. I said that Captain Grimes was my brother and the Marine's face lit up. He described the outstanding medical care and real compassion that Sean had provided for the Marines wounded in combat, who were brought to the Field Hospital on Sean's base camp. It was a sad moment when I answered the Marine's question about where

Sean was serving now. His eyes began fill with tears and he slowly shook his head saying:

"Captain Grimes was a great, great man. He really took care of my Marines".

CPT Sean P. Grimes 4 Mar 2005
PL Stephen M. McGowan 4 Mar 2005
SPC Wade M. Twyman 4 Mar 2005

Sean finally made it to Ft. Carson. Here is his name on the memorial outside the main gate.

Chapter 19

Sean almost always had a smile on his face and a word of encouragement and support for everyone he met. He knew the importance of being around people who shared his positive values and positive outlook. The soldiers he was with, in that final moment when the bomb ended his life, had helped him be the great man he was. Sergeant First Class Don Eacho, Corporal Stephen McGowan and Specialist Wade Twyman were soldiers whom Sean liked, respected and loved and he felt honored to be serving with them. And he felt honored that they liked and respected him, too, and considered him to be "one of the Scouts".

My brother had a laser-like focus on always improving his medical skills and on using those skills as often as possible, to help as many people as possible. In Iraq, Sean also provided medical care for Iraqi soldiers and civilians and even to terrorists who had killed and wounded his friends. I see now, that I have often lacked the single-mindedness that Sean had.

Sean had a vibrant love for life. He died very young, but he certainly packed a lifetime of joy, love and excitement into his short life. I realize and regret that I have not always lived with the same sense of joy and wonder that underpinned Sean's adult life.

Sean had a quiet type of strength, courage and character. In his world of soldiering and medicine he was *hot stuff* and on the fast track, but he understood that real leaders have a quiet strength and a servant's heart. Before he left for Iraq, I was bragging about him to some friends of mine we had run into in a local store. Afterwards, when Sean and I were alone in my car he said to me,

"I'm glad you're proud of me but I'm just a soldier. Just like all the other soldiers".

How refreshing and rare is this kind of humility in our society today.

Chapter 20

Life of Captain Sean Grimes, RN, PA-C, U.S. Army

1. We all start life in different circumstances. Some have an ideal upbringing, some are raised in chaos and most people are somewhere in-between. Where we start in life does not have to determine where we end up – nor dictate the kind of life we live as an adult.

2. Creating joy, meaning and success in our life can be helped by associating with quality people, and the opposite is definitely true, too!
    Who are you associating with? Are you a better person for spending time with them? Do they encourage you to take action towards achieving your dreams?

3. Finding true love can take a while. We cannot predict where we will find the right person and smart people do not try to force it.
    Take your time to live a bit and then figure out what you want in a partner. Then stay open to possibilities.

4. You will spend most of your waking hours at your job, so take personal responsibility for finding your true calling.

5. When you find your vocation, don't stop until you reach your full potential. Be willing to work very hard and sometimes make sacrifices that others on a similar path would not be willing to make. Laying down good foundations will help you to build a satisfying career *and* get the most out of every aspect of your life!

6. Be a person of strong character: honest, kind, hard working and loyal to your friends, co-workers and the organizations and groups to which you belong. People of character are rare today and you will be always be highly valued by good people if you are one.

7. Leadership means giving strong positive guidance, actively taking responsibility for the welfare of your team and holding your people responsible for their actions. Sometimes leaders have to make unpopular decisions.

8. Staying focused on becoming outstanding at your job does not mean you cannot have fun. Have fun!

9. Real joy comes from service and helping others achieve their dreams. Encourage others whenever you can and take a real interest in them.

10. Life flies by!

Chapter 21

My sister Mary and I have established two scholarships in honor of Sean's life and achievements which are awarded to veterans/active members of: the Army, the Army Reserve or the Army National Guard.

The scholarship at Michigan State University is for the School of Nursing. The other scholarship is for study to become a Physician Assistant at any approved PA program in the U.S. and is administered by the Society of Army Physician Assistants and the Physician Assistant Foundation. We have also donated funds towards the creation of the: **'Captain Sean Grimes PA Training Center' at Ft. Campbell, KY**

We felt very honored and proud to discover that the students at the Jefferson College of Health Sciences (JCHS) Physician Assistant (PA) Program had named their student association: **'The Captain Sean Grimes Student Society of the Jefferson College of Health Sciences (JCHS) Physician Assistant (PA) Program'**

Sean was a proud graduate of the U.S. Army ROTC training program. He attended training at Ft. Lewis, Washington. In 2007, the U.S. Army ROTC at Ft. Lewis, WA, honored his memory by naming their First Aid Course, **'The Captain Sean Grimes 1st Aid Course'**.

*The sign beside the new **Captain Sean Grimes PA Training Center** at Ft. Campbell, KY*

*My son Scott, Sean's nephew, at the dedication of the **Captain Sean Grimes PA Training Center**
at Madigan Army Medical Center at Ft. Campbell, KY*

Made in the USA
Charleston, SC
22 April 2012